KT-380-537

Look out on the Road

17.

1/

RED RAINBOWS

The Caterpillar Story
Houses and Homes
Look out at Home
Look out by Water
Look out for Strangers
Look out on the Road*
Looking Around
My Senses
Old and New
Sun's Hot, Sea's Cold
What People Do

What's the Weather?
When Dad was Young
When Grandma was Young
My Christian Faith*
Fy Fydd Gristnogol (Welsh edition)*
My Hindu Faith*
My Jewish Faith*
My Muslim Faith*
My Sikh Faith*
My Buddhist Faith*
*Also available as Big Books

EDUCATIONAL AND READING CONSULTANT

Diana Bentley and Dee Reid, Senior Lecturers in Language and Reading,
Oxford Brookes University

SAFETY CONSULTANT

Checked by the Safety Advisor at the Royal Society for the Prevention of
Accidents (RoSPA), RoSPA House, Edgbaston Park, 353 Bristol Road,
Birmingham B5 7ST
Reprinted 2007

Published by Evans Brothers Limited
2A Portman Mansions
Chiltern Street
London W1U 6NR

First published in paperback in 2003

Printed in China by WKT Co. Ltd.

ISBN 978 0 237 52542 2

ACKNOWLEDGEMENTS
Planned and produced by Paul Humphrey
Picture Research by Helena Ramsay
Designed by Ian Winton
Tyesetting by Gamecock Graphics

For permission to reproduce copyright material the author and publishers
gratefully acknowledge the following:
Chris Fairclough Colour Library: all other pictures.
The publishers would also like to thank the
Ludlow Bike Centre for the loan of the bicycles shown in the book.

Look out on the Road

Paul Humphrey and
Alex Ramsay

Illustrated by
Colin King

Evans

We're going shopping and then we can go for a walk in the country.

We're in the car.

Here we are at the shops.

Always hold a grown-up's
hand, then you will be safe.

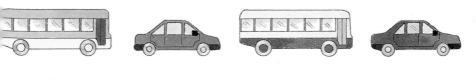

Always be careful when you are near a road.

The edge of the pavement
is called the kerb.
Never stand too close
to the kerb.

Let's look for a safe place to cross the road.
Here is a pelican crossing.

Can I press the button?

12

PEDESTRIANS
push button and wait
for signal opposite

WAIT

cross
with care

do not start
to cross

wait

FLASHING

13

Now we must wait for the signal before we cross the road.

14

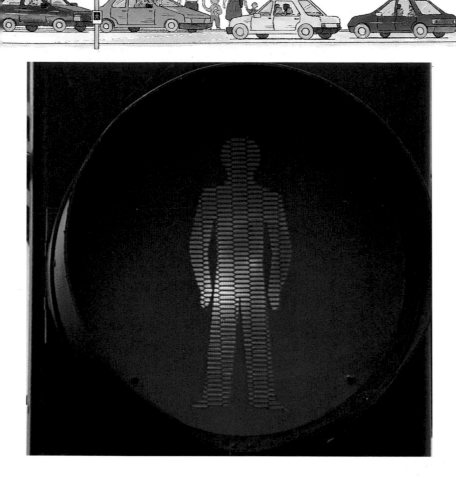

The red man shows us
that it's not safe to cross
the road.

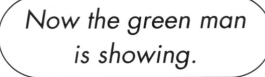

Now the green man is showing.

And the cars have stopped for us.

It's safe to go across now.

16

Be sure to go on looking and
listening while you cross
the road.

17

There are other safe places
to cross the road.

The lollipop lady at school
stops the traffic.

Policemen sometimes help
people to cross the road.

19

A helmet will protect his head
if he falls off his bike.

A shiny belt helps car drivers to see him easily.

He is showing other people
on the road that he wants to
turn left.

25

26

Always walk on the
right-hand side of the
road so that you can see,
and be seen by, the traffic.

Can you remember
the rules for crossing
the road
safely?

Always STOP
at the kerb.

LOOK out for traffic.

28

Keep LOOKING and
LISTENING as you cross.

Look at this picture. Some of the people are being sensible and some are being silly. Which are which?

Index